PACMAN FROG CARE GUIDE FOR BEGINNERS

Expert Tips On Pet Amphibian Habitat Setup, Horned Frog Handling, Species, Diet, Health, Breeding, Tank Maintenance, Substrate, Humidity, Lighting, hydration.

ETHAN HARRY

Table of Contents

CHAPTER ONE 6
- **INTRODUCTION TO PACMAN FROGS** 6
  - Overview Of Pacman Frogs 8
  - Understanding Their Natural Habitat 11
  - Why Choose A Pacman Frog As A Pet? 14

CHAPTER TWO 17
- **SELECTING A PACMAN FROG** 17
  - Choosing The Right Species 17
  - Healthy Vs. Unhealthy Frogs: What To Look For 20
  - Where To Buy Your Pacman Frog 22

CHAPTER THREE 26
- **SETTING UP THE HABITAT** 26
  - Ideal Tank Size And Type 26
  - Substrate Options 28
  - Decorations And Hiding Spots 31
  - Temperature And Humidity Requirements 34
  - Lighting And Uvb Needs 36

CHAPTER FOUR 39
- **FEEDING YOUR PACMAN FROG** 39
  - Understanding Their Diet 39
  - Feeding Schedule 42
  - Live Vs. Prey Items 44
  - Vitamin And Mineral Supplements 46

CHAPTER FIVE 49

WATER AND HYDRATION 49
Importance Of Clean Water 49

Maintaining Proper Humidity Levels 51

Signs Of Dehydration 53

CHAPTER SIX 57

HANDLING AND INTERACTION 57
Safe Handling Techniques 57

How Often Should You Handle Your Frog? 59

Recognizing Stress In Your Frog 61

CHAPTER SEVEN 65

HEALTH AND WELLNESS 65
Common Health Issues 65

Signs Of A Healthy Frog 67

Preventative Care 70

CHAPTER EIGHT 73

DEALING WITH ILLNESS 73
Recognizing Early Signs Of Illness 73

Common Diseases And Treatments 75

When To See A Veterinarian 78

CHAPTER NINE 81

BREEDING PACMAN FROGS 81
Understanding Breeding Behavior 81

Setting Up A Breeding Tank 83

Caring For Eggs And Tadpoles 87

CHAPTER TEN 89

3

SEASONAL CARE AND ADJUSTMENTS 89
Adapting To Different Seasons 89

Winter Care: Hibernation And Brumation 92

Summer Care: Heat And Hydration 95

CHAPTER ELEVEN 101

TANK MAINTENANCE 101
Regular Cleaning Schedule 101

Managing Mold And Fungus 103

Safe Handling Of Waste And Uneaten Food 106

CHAPTER TWELVE 109

ENRICHMENT AND STIMULATION 109
Environmental Enrichment 109

Mental Stimulation Techniques 111

Creating A Naturalistic Environment 114

CHAPTER THIRTEEN 117

TRAVELING WITH YOUR PACMAN FROG 117
Preparing For Travel 117

Ensuring Safety During Transit 119

Post-Travel Care 122

CHAPTER FOURTEEN 125

LEGAL AND ETHICAL CONSIDERATIONS 125
Understanding Local Laws And Regulations 125

Ethical Care Practices 127

The Importance Of Captive Breeding 130

CHAPTER FIFTEEN 133

TROUBLESHOOTING AND FAQS 133
Common Beginner Mistakes 133
Frequently Asked Questions 137
THE END 142

CHAPTER ONE

INTRODUCTION TO PACMAN FROGS

Pacman frogs, also called horned frogs, are a unique and interesting type of amphibian that many people enjoy keeping as pets. Their name comes from their large, round bodies and wide mouths. This fun appearance is just one of the many reasons why Pacman frogs have become so popular among reptile and amphibian lovers.

These frogs are native to South America, where they can be found in countries like Argentina, Brazil, and Paraguay. They live in humid, tropical environments, which is why they prefer warm and moist conditions in captivity. Pacman frogs are known for their ability to burrow into the ground, often hiding themselves almost completely from view. This helps them stay cool and safe in the wild, and it's something they do often when kept as pets.

One of the most fascinating things about Pacman frogs is their size. They can grow quite large compared to other frogs, with some reaching up to 7 inches in diameter. Their large size is matched by their big appetite. Pacman frogs are ambush predators, which means they like to sit and wait for their prey to come close before they strike. They eat a variety of foods, including insects, small rodents, and even other frogs. Their feeding habits are part of what makes them so interesting to watch.

Despite their fierce appearance and eating habits, Pacman frogs are relatively easy to care for. They don't need a lot of space, and they are not very active, which makes them a good choice for people who want a low-maintenance pet. However, it's important to remember that they can live for 10-15 years, so taking on the responsibility of caring for a Pacman frog is a long-term commitment.

In addition to their physical appearance, Pacman frogs are known for their vocalizations. Males, in particular, can make loud, croaking sounds, especially during the breeding season. These sounds are part of their natural behavior and are one of the many ways they communicate with each other.

Overview Of Pacman Frogs

Pacman frogs, also known as frogs of the genus Ceratophrys, are native to South America. They got their name because of their big, round mouths, which they use to catch and eat prey. These frogs are famous for their big appetites and will eat almost anything that fits in their mouths, including mice, birds, and even other frogs. Their large mouths and round bodies give them a distinctive look that makes them easy to recognize.

There are several types of Pacman frogs, but the ones most often kept as pets are the Argentine horned frog (Ceratophrys ornata) and Cranwell's horned frog (Ceratophrys cranwelli). Both of these species have similar needs when it comes to care and behavior, which makes them popular pets for people who want to keep an unusual amphibian.

Pacman frogs come in different colors and patterns. You can find them in shades of green, brown, and yellow, often with detailed markings that help them blend into their surroundings. Despite their bright and interesting looks, Pacman frogs are ambush predators. This means they stay still and use their camouflage to hide from their prey, waiting for the right moment to strike.

Caring for a Pacman frog is relatively straightforward, but there are a few things to keep in mind. They need a warm and humid environment that mimics their natural habitat in the tropical rainforests of South America. A proper diet is also essential; since Pacman frogs have such large appetites, they need plenty of food, such as crickets, worms, and sometimes even small mice. However, it's important not to overfeed them, as they can easily become overweight.

Pacman frogs are solitary creatures and prefer to be alone. They do not require much interaction and can be stressed if handled too often. These frogs spend most of their time buried in the substrate of their enclosure, with only their eyes visible, waiting for prey to come close. Because of their sedentary lifestyle, they don't need a large enclosure, but they do need one that's kept clean and properly maintained.

Understanding Their Natural Habitat

To take good care of a Pacman frog, it's important to know about its natural habitat. Pacman frogs come from the humid, tropical areas of South America, mainly in countries like Argentina, Brazil, and Paraguay. These frogs like to live in places with lots of plants, where the air is very humid, and there are plenty of spots for them to hide and hunt.

Pacman frogs are terrestrial, meaning they spend most of their time on the ground rather than in water. In the wild, they are usually found in areas with soft, moist soil. They use this soil to burrow, which helps them escape the heat during the day or hide from predators. The high humidity of their natural environment is very important for their survival. It keeps their skin moist and helps them absorb water.

When you keep a Pacman frog as a pet, it's crucial to create a home for it that mimics its natural habitat. Start by setting up a tank with a substrate that allows the frog to burrow. Good options include coconut fiber or sphagnum moss. These materials hold moisture well, making them ideal for maintaining the high humidity levels that the frog needs.

To keep the humidity high, you should mist the tank regularly with water. A humidity level of around 70% to 80% is ideal for Pacman frogs. You can use a hygrometer, which is a tool that measures humidity, to make sure the levels are right. If the humidity drops too low, the frog's skin can dry out, which can lead to health problems.

In addition to humidity, your Pacman frog will need a shallow water dish in its tank. The dish should be big enough for the frog to sit in but not so deep that it could have trouble getting out. This water dish helps the frog stay hydrated, and the water should be changed regularly to keep it clean.

Lastly, make sure the tank has plenty of hiding spots. You can use pieces of bark, plants, or small caves. These hiding spots help the frog feel secure and comfortable, just like it would in the wild.

Why Choose A Pacman Frog As A Pet?

Pacman frogs make great pets for several reasons. First, their unique look makes them stand out from other amphibians. They have big mouths, round bodies, and bright colors, making them eye-catching and interesting to have as pets.

One of the best things about Pacman frogs is that they are easy to care for. Unlike some other reptiles and amphibians, they don't need a large tank or complicated equipment. A simple tank with the right bedding, humidity, and temperature is enough to keep them healthy and happy. Pacman frogs are also not very active, so they don't need much space to move around, which makes them ideal for people who may not have a lot of room for a pet.

Another fascinating aspect of Pacman frogs is their behavior. These frogs are ambush predators, which means they spend most of their time hiding in the substrate, waiting for prey to come close. When they do strike, it's quick and powerful, making feeding time an exciting event to watch. This unique behavior adds to their charm and makes them an interesting pet to observe.

However, it's important to know that Pacman frogs are not the best pets for handling. Their skin is very sensitive, and they can become stressed if they are handled too much. This makes them better suited for owners who prefer to watch their pets rather than interact with them directly. If you're someone who enjoys observing animals in their natural behavior, a Pacman frog could be the perfect pet for you.

CHAPTER TWO

SELECTING A PACMAN FROG

Choosing The Right Species

When deciding on a Pacman frog as a pet, it's important to choose the right species for your needs and experience level. Pacman frogs, also known as horned frogs, come in a few different species, each with its own special traits. The three most popular species kept as pets are the Argentine Horned Frog (Ceratophrys ornata), the Cranwell's Horned Frog (Ceratophrys cranwelli), and the Fantasy Horned Frog, a hybrid of the first two.

The Argentine Horned Frog is famous for its bright and vibrant colors, which can include shades of green, red, and orange. These frogs can grow quite large, often reaching about 6 to 7 inches in length.

Their striking appearance and relatively easy care requirements make them a great choice for beginners who are interested in a colorful pet that's not too difficult to manage.

Next is the Cranwell's Horned Frog, which is usually less colorful than the Argentine Horned Frog. This species often has more muted, earthy tones like browns and greens, but they are still very attractive. One of the main advantages of the Cranwell's Horned Frog is that it tends to be more hardy and resilient, which makes it an excellent choice for those who are new to caring for frogs. If you're looking for a tough and easy-going pet, this might be the best species for you.

Finally, there's the Fantasy Horned Frog, a unique hybrid between the Argentine and

Cranwell's species. This frog can display a wide range of colors and patterns, making it visually appealing and unique. Fantasy Horned Frogs are generally a bit smaller than their purebred relatives, but they are just as fascinating to keep. Because they are a mix of two species, they can vary quite a bit in appearance, which might appeal to those who want a more distinctive pet.

When choosing which Pacman frog to bring home, think about what you want in a pet. Consider the size, color, and personality you prefer, as well as your experience level with amphibians. If you're new to owning frogs, the Cranwell's Horned Frog could be the best choice due to its hardiness and ease of care. However, if you're drawn to bright colors and don't mind a slightly larger pet, the Argentine Horned Frog might be more your style. The Fantasy Horned Frog offers a unique middle ground with its mix of traits from both parent species.

Healthy Vs. Unhealthy Frogs: What To Look For

When choosing a Pacman frog, it's essential to pick a healthy one to ensure it thrives in your care. Here's a simple guide to help you spot the signs of a healthy versus an unhealthy frog.

First, pay attention to the frog's behavior. Pacman frogs are naturally lazy and like to stay still, but a healthy frog should still react to movement, sounds, or food. If the frog seems overly still, sluggish, or doesn't respond when you approach it, it might not be in good health.

Next, check the frog's eyes. Healthy Pacman frogs have clear, bright eyes. If the eyes look cloudy, dull, or if there's any discharge, it could be a sign that the frog is sick or dehydrated. Good eye health is a strong indicator of the frog's overall well-being.

The condition of the frog's skin is another important factor. Healthy Pacman frogs have smooth, moist skin without any cuts, sores, or infections. When inspecting the skin, look for any unusual bumps, discoloration, or peeling. These could be signs of skin diseases or other health issues that might require attention.

Also, observe the frog's body shape. A healthy Pacman frog should have a plump, rounded body, showing that it is well-fed. However, it shouldn't look bloated, as this could indicate internal problems. On the other hand, a frog that appears too thin might not be getting enough food or could be dealing with malnutrition.

Finally, examine the vent area, which is located on the underside of the frog near the tail. This area should be clean, with no signs of swelling, redness, or discharge. Problems in this area could suggest digestive issues or parasites, which can severely affect the frog's health.

Where To Buy Your Pacman Frog

When it comes to buying a Pacman frog, choosing the right place is important to ensure you get a healthy pet. There are three main options: pet stores, breeders, and online retailers. Each has its pros and cons, so it's essential to make an informed decision.

Pet Stores

Many pet stores sell Pacman frogs, but the care they receive can vary. When visiting a pet store, take a close look at how the frogs are kept. The enclosure should be clean, with the right humidity levels, and the frogs should have enough space. Avoid stores where the frogs are overcrowded or the tanks are dirty, as this could indicate poor care. Also, pay attention to the staff; they should be knowledgeable and able to answer your questions about the frogs.

Breeders

Buying from a breeder is often the best option. Breeders usually have more experience and knowledge about Pacman frogs and can provide detailed information about their care. A good breeder can tell you about the frog's health, age, and even its family history. They are also more likely to have a variety of species and colors (morphs) to choose from. When dealing with a breeder, ask questions about how they care for their frogs and what you can expect when you bring yours home.

Online Retailers

Buying a Pacman frog online is convenient, especially if you're looking for a specific type. However, it's crucial to do your research. Look for online sellers with good reviews and a reputation for taking care of their animals. Make sure the retailer offers a live arrival guarantee, which means they promise your frog will arrive healthy and alive. Also, check their return policy in case the frog isn't in good condition when it arrives.

No matter where you decide to buy your Pacman frog, always ask the seller questions about the frog's age, health, and current care routine. A trustworthy seller will be happy to provide this information. Taking the time to choose the right place to buy your frog will help ensure you bring home a healthy, well-cared-for pet.

CHAPTER THREE

SETTING UP THE HABITAT

Ideal Tank Size And Type

Pacman Frogs, known for their impressive size and laid-back nature, need a spacious tank to live comfortably. An adult Pacman Frog thrives best in a 20-gallon long tank. This size offers plenty of room for the frog to move around and helps keep the environment stable, which is essential for its health and well-being.

For young Pacman Frogs, you can start with a smaller tank, but you'll need to upgrade it as the frog grows. A 20-gallon long tank is a good choice for an adult because it provides enough space for the frog to stretch out and explore, even though Pacman Frogs are not very active.

When choosing a tank, opt for one made of glass or acrylic. Both materials are clear, making it easy to see your frog, and are simple to clean. It's important to make sure the tank has a secure lid. Pacman Frogs are not known for climbing, so you don't need a tank with high sides, but the lid will prevent your frog from escaping, as they can be quite adept at finding their way out if given the chance.

In addition to the tank itself, consider the layout inside. Pacman Frogs prefer a low, wide setup rather than a tall, narrow one. They spend most of their time sitting still rather than climbing or jumping, so a tank that provides ample ground space is more suitable than one with vertical space.

Maintaining stable environmental conditions is crucial for these frogs. The larger tank size helps in maintaining proper humidity and temperature levels, which are vital for their health. Ensure the tank has a proper substrate, such as damp soil or moss, and a shallow water dish where the frog can soak. Regularly check the tank's conditions and clean it as needed to provide a healthy living environment.

Substrate Options

When setting up a habitat for a Pacman Frog, choosing the right substrate is essential. The substrate is the material that lines the bottom of the enclosure, and it needs to be soft, moist, and capable of retaining humidity. Here are some of the best options:

1. Coconut Fiber

Coconut fiber is a top choice for Pacman Frog enclosures. It is excellent at holding moisture, which is crucial for maintaining the high humidity levels that Pacman Frogs need. This substrate is also easy to clean, making it convenient for regular maintenance. Additionally, coconut fiber gives the enclosure a natural look, which can help make your frog feel more at home. It is also a sustainable option, as it is made from the husks of coconuts.

2. Sphagnum Moss

Sphagnum moss is another great substrate for Pacman Frogs. This material is particularly effective at maintaining high humidity levels, which is beneficial for the frog's health. Sphagnum moss is soft and comfortable for the frog to burrow into, offering a suitable environment for its natural behaviors. It also has natural antimicrobial properties, which can help reduce the risk of mold and bacteria growth in the enclosure.

3. Topsoil

Natural topsoil can also be used as a substrate, but there are a few important considerations. It must be free of fertilizers, pesticides, and other chemicals that could be harmful to the frog. To improve moisture retention and create a more suitable environment, topsoil can be mixed with coconut fiber or sphagnum moss. This blend helps to maintain the right humidity levels and creates a more natural and comfortable habitat for the frog.

When selecting a substrate, it's important to avoid materials that can be harmful to the frog. For example, sand or gravel should be avoided as they do not retain moisture well and can cause health problems if ingested. Always choose substrates that are easy to clean and replace as needed, ensuring that the Pacman Frog's habitat remains healthy and comfortable.

Decorations And Hiding Spots

Pacman Frogs are naturally burrowing creatures and need hiding spots to feel safe and secure in their habitat. To create a comfortable environment for your frog, it's important to include decorations that mimic their natural surroundings and provide plenty of places for them to hide and explore.

Cork Bark: Cork bark is a great material to use in your frog's enclosure. It can be placed flat on the substrate to create a hiding spot that looks like the frog's natural habitat. Cork bark not only provides a secure place for the frog to retreat but also adds a natural, rustic look to the setup. The texture of cork bark is perfect for helping the frog feel safe and hidden, just like it would in the wild.

Artificial Plants: Adding artificial plants to the enclosure is another way to make it more inviting and interesting for your Pacman Frog. Fake plants can provide extra hiding spots and make the environment look more natural. When choosing artificial plants, select ones that are easy to clean and won't break down or deteriorate in the high humidity typical of a frog's habitat. This ensures that the plants will last longer and continue to serve their purpose of providing cover and visual enrichment for your frog.

Hollow Logs or Caves: Incorporating hollow logs or caves into the enclosure creates additional hiding spaces for your Pacman Frog. These can be made from various materials, such as plastic or natural wood, and should be large enough for the frog to comfortably enter and exit. Hollow logs and caves offer a private retreat for the frog to hide and feel secure, which is essential for their well-being.

When setting up your frog's habitat, make sure to arrange these decorations in a way that allows easy access and movement for the frog. Avoid overcrowding the enclosure, as your Pacman Frog needs enough space to move around comfortably.

Temperature And Humidity Requirements

Keeping your Pacman Frog healthy involves maintaining the right temperature and humidity levels in its habitat. Here's what you need to know to create the best environment for your frog.

Temperature: Pacman Frogs are happiest in temperatures between 75-80°F (24-27°C). This temperature range is similar to their natural tropical habitat. To achieve and maintain this temperature range, use an aquarium heater or a heat pad. Place the heat pad under one side of the tank. This setup creates a temperature gradient, allowing your frog to move between warmer and cooler areas as needed. It's important not to place the heater directly inside the tank. This can cause burns or make the environment too hot in one spot. Regularly check the temperature with a reliable thermometer to ensure it stays within the ideal range.

Humidity: High humidity is crucial for the health of your Pacman Frog. Aim to keep the humidity level between 60-80%. This high humidity helps mimic the damp conditions of their natural environment. To maintain these humidity levels, mist the tank regularly. You can also use a humidifier to add moisture to the air if needed. The substrate in the tank should be kept moist, but it should not be waterlogged. If the substrate is too wet, it can lead to mold growth and other issues.

To monitor the humidity levels accurately, use a hygrometer. This tool measures the amount of moisture in the air and helps you keep the environment within the desired range. By regularly misting the tank and using a hygrometer, you can ensure your Pacman Frog's habitat remains comfortable and healthy.

Lighting And Uvb Needs

Pacman Frogs are nocturnal creatures, which means they are active mostly at night. Because of this, they don't need strong lighting like some other pets. However, having a natural light cycle in their habitat can help keep them healthy and happy.

Lighting

For Pacman Frogs, you don't need anything too bright. A simple, low-wattage fluorescent light or an LED light works perfectly. Set it on a 12-hour on and 12-hour off cycle. This means the light should be on for 12 hours a day and off for 12 hours at night. This mimics the natural day and night cycle, helping your frog maintain its natural rhythm.

Avoid placing the tank in direct sunlight. Direct sunlight can cause the tank to overheat, which can stress out your frog and disrupt its natural behavior. The light in the tank should be gentle enough that it doesn't disturb your frog's nighttime activities.

UVB Lighting

Pacman Frogs do not need UVB lighting. UVB lights are often used for reptiles and amphibians that need extra help absorbing vitamin D3 from the sun, but Pacman Frogs get enough vitamin D3 from their diet. Their natural diet provides all the nutrients they need to stay healthy.

If you decide to use UVB lighting, choose a bulb with low output. This means the UVB light shouldn't be too strong, as Pacman Frogs are not used to high levels of UVB exposure. Also, make sure to provide shaded areas in the tank where your frog can escape from the UVB light. This way, your frog can choose to be in the light or in the shade according to its needs.

CHAPTER FOUR

FEEDING YOUR PACMAN FROG

Understanding Their Diet

Pacman frogs are meat-eaters with specific dietary needs. In their natural habitat, they consume a variety of foods, including insects, small vertebrates, and sometimes other small animals. When kept as pets, it's important to provide them with a diet that closely resembles what they would eat in the wild. This helps ensure they get all the essential nutrients they need to stay healthy.

A Pacman frog's diet should be diverse, including the following key components:

1. Crickets: Crickets are a fundamental part of a Pacman frog's diet. They should be provided regularly as they are a primary source of food and nutrition. Crickets are

easily available and can be purchased from pet stores. Ensure that the crickets are appropriately sized for your frog to prevent any potential choking hazards.

2. Mealworms: Mealworms are another good food choice for Pacman frogs. However, they should be given in moderation. While mealworms are nutritious, they are also high in fat, which can lead to obesity if fed in excess. Offering mealworms once or twice a week is a good practice to maintain a balanced diet.

3. Roaches: Dubia roaches are highly nutritious and make an excellent addition to your Pacman frog's diet. They are rich in protein and other essential nutrients that help keep your frog healthy. Dubia roaches are easy to care for and breed, making

them a practical choice for feeding your frog.

4. Worms: Earthworms and silk worms are also beneficial for Pacman frogs. They provide a good source of protein and other nutrients. Earthworms are particularly valuable as they help with digestion and provide essential vitamins and minerals. Silk worms are a tasty treat that adds variety to their diet.

In addition to offering these foods, it's crucial to maintain a varied diet to ensure your Pacman frog receives a complete range of nutrients. A balanced diet helps prevent nutritional deficiencies and promotes overall health. It's also important to provide appropriate supplements, such as calcium and vitamins, to ensure your frog's diet is well-rounded.

Feeding Schedule

Maintaining a regular feeding schedule is essential for the health and well-being of your Pacman frog. Whether your frog is young or an adult, their feeding needs vary. Here's a simple guide to help you feed your Pacman frog properly.

Juvenile Pacman Frogs (up to 6 months old): These young frogs are growing quickly, so they need more frequent feedings. To support their rapid growth and high metabolism, you should feed them every 2 to 3 days. This ensures they get enough nutrients to develop properly. You can offer them small live insects like crickets or worms, which are perfect for their size and dietary needs.

Adult Pacman Frogs (over 6 months old): As Pacman frogs mature, their metabolism slows down. Consequently, their feeding schedule changes. For adult Pacman frogs, feeding once or twice a week is sufficient. They do not need to eat as often as juveniles because they have a slower metabolism. Adult frogs can eat larger insects, such as big crickets or small mice, depending on their size and preference.

By following these guidelines, you'll help your Pacman frog stay healthy and happy. Regular feeding helps maintain their energy levels, supports their growth, and keeps them active. It's also important to monitor their weight and adjust their food intake if necessary. Overfeeding can lead to obesity, while underfeeding can result in malnutrition.

Always provide clean, fresh water for your Pacman frog to drink. Hydration is just as important as proper feeding. Make sure their habitat is clean and their food is fresh to avoid any health issues. If you notice any changes in your frog's eating habits or health, consult a veterinarian who specializes in reptiles and amphibians.

Live Vs. Prey Items

Pacman frogs in captivity can eat both live and pre-killed food, but each option has its own pros and cons.

Live Prey

Feeding your Pacman frog live prey, like crickets or worms, is great because it helps keep their natural hunting instincts sharp. Chasing and capturing live food provides mental stimulation and encourages exercise, which can be beneficial for their overall health. However, live prey comes with some risks. It might carry diseases or parasites that could harm your frog. To minimize these risks, always get live prey from reliable suppliers who take good care of their insects or worms.

When offering live prey, it's crucial to ensure the food is the right size. The prey should be no larger than the width of your frog's head. If the food is too big, your frog might struggle to eat it or could choke.

Pre-Killed Prey

On the other hand, pre-killed prey, such as frozen-thawed mice, is a convenient alternative. This type of food is often safer because it reduces the risk of parasites or diseases being introduced to your frog. When using pre-killed prey, make sure it is completely thawed and warmed before feeding. Cold or frozen food might not appeal to your frog and could be less nutritious.

Feeding Tips

Whether you choose live or pre-killed prey, remember that the food should always be appropriately sized for your frog. The safety and health of your Pacman frog depend on offering the right portion sizes and ensuring the food is safe to eat.

Vitamin And Mineral Supplements

To keep your Pacman frog healthy and thriving, it's important to provide the right vitamin and mineral supplements. These supplements help prevent nutritional deficiencies and support your frog's overall well-being. Here's a simple guide to what your Pacman frog needs:

Calcium: Calcium is essential for your Pacman frog's bone health and various metabolic functions. Without enough calcium, your frog could develop serious health issues. To make sure your frog gets enough calcium, use a calcium powder supplement. Dust this powder onto the prey items before feeding them to your frog. This is especially important if you have a young frog or a female that is breeding, as their calcium needs are higher.

Vitamin D3: Vitamin D3 is crucial because it helps your frog absorb calcium properly. Many calcium supplements already contain Vitamin D3, but if yours doesn't, you might need to provide it separately. Vitamin D3 ensures that the calcium your frog consumes is used effectively by their body.

Multivitamins: Multivitamins are another important part of your frog's diet. A reptile-specific multivitamin provides a range of essential vitamins and minerals that your frog needs for good health. However, you don't need to give multivitamins as often as calcium. Offering a multivitamin once every 1-2 weeks is usually sufficient.

CHAPTER FIVE

WATER AND HYDRATION

Importance Of Clean Water

Pacman Frogs are native to moist, tropical environments where water plays a crucial role in their daily lives. To keep these unique amphibians healthy in captivity, it's essential to provide them with a clean and constant supply of water. Here's why clean water is so important:

1. Hydration:

Pacman Frogs absorb water through their skin, which means they need access to clean water at all times. Unlike humans and other animals that drink water through their mouths, these frogs take in moisture directly through their skin. If the water they have access to becomes stagnant or dirty, it can lead to serious health problems. Dirty water can cause skin infections, which can be uncomfortable and potentially harmful to the frog's overall well-being. To prevent such issues, ensure that the water in their habitat is always fresh and clean.

2. Temperature Regulation:

Water also plays a key role in helping Pacman Frogs regulate their body temperature. In their natural habitat, the temperature around them is usually stable and conducive to their health. If the water in their enclosure is too warm or too cold, it can affect their health. Proper temperature regulation is essential for maintaining their normal bodily functions. Keeping the water at the right temperature helps ensure that the frog remains comfortable and can maintain its natural metabolic processes.

3. Digestion:

Hydration is crucial for digestion in Pacman Frogs. These frogs often eat their prey whole, and having enough water in their system helps in breaking down the food efficiently. Adequate hydration aids in the digestive process, making it easier for them to process their food and absorb nutrients. Without proper hydration, the digestion process can be hindered, potentially leading to digestive issues and discomfort.

Maintaining Proper Humidity Levels

Humidity is essential for keeping Pacman Frogs healthy. These frogs come from rainforest environments where the air is moist, so their habitat needs to mimic these conditions. Here's how to keep the humidity levels just right:

1. Humidity Range: Pacman Frogs thrive in a humidity range of 60% to 80%. This range is similar to the moist air in their natural rainforest homes. To keep them comfortable, you need to ensure that the humidity in their enclosure stays within this range.

2. Substrate: The material at the bottom of the enclosure, known as substrate, plays a big role in maintaining humidity. Use substrates that hold moisture well, like coconut fiber or sphagnum moss. These materials help keep the air moist and provide a comfortable environment for the frogs. Make sure the substrate is damp, but not soaking wet.

3. Enclosure: To keep the air inside the enclosure moist, regularly mist the inside with a spray bottle. Alternatively, you can use an automatic misting system for convenience. Keep an eye on the humidity levels with a hygrometer, a device that measures humidity, to make sure they stay within the ideal 60% to 80% range.

4. Water Dish: The water dish in the enclosure also helps with humidity. Ensure that the dish is large enough to contribute to moisture levels and keep it filled with fresh water. The presence of water in the dish will help increase the humidity in the air, benefiting your Pacman Frogs.

Signs Of Dehydration

Keeping an eye on your Pacman Frog's health is essential, and one key aspect is ensuring they are properly hydrated.

Dehydration can lead to serious health issues, so it's important to know the signs and take action quickly if you spot them. Here's a guide to help you recognize dehydration in your Pacman Frog:

1. Dull or Dry Skin: A healthy Pacman Frog has smooth and moist skin. If you notice that your frog's skin looks dull or feels dry to the touch, this might be a sign of dehydration. The skin should be soft and shiny, not rough or flaky.

2. Sunken Eyes: Another common sign of dehydration is when a frog's eyes appear sunken or recessed into their sockets. Healthy frogs usually have eyes that are full and round. If the eyes seem to be sinking in, it could indicate that the frog is not getting enough water.

3. Lethargy: If your Pacman Frog seems unusually tired or less active than usual, it might be suffering from dehydration. Frogs that are well-hydrated are typically more lively and alert. If your frog is staying in one place for long periods or not moving around much, it's worth checking for other signs of dehydration.

4. Difficulty Shedding: Dehydration can also affect your frog's ability to shed its skin properly. If you notice that your frog is having trouble shedding or if there are pieces of old skin stuck to its body, it might need more moisture in its environment. Proper shedding is essential for a healthy frog, and difficulty with this process can be a clear sign of dehydration.

If you spot any of these signs, it's important to act quickly. Start by increasing the humidity in your frog's enclosure. Ensure that the water dish is clean and always filled with fresh water. You might also want to mist the habitat more frequently to add moisture to the environment.

If you have made these changes and the symptoms persist, it's a good idea to consult a veterinarian who specializes in amphibians. They can provide further advice and treatment to ensure your Pacman Frog stays healthy and hydrated.

CHAPTER SIX

HANDLING AND INTERACTION

Safe Handling Techniques

Handling your Pacman frog properly is essential for keeping both you and your frog safe. Pacman frogs can be sensitive, so it's important to use the right techniques to ensure their well-being and avoid causing stress.

1. Wash Your Hands: Before touching your Pacman frog, wash your hands thoroughly. This removes oils, dirt, and chemicals that could harm your frog. Make sure to use a mild, fragrance-free soap, as strong fragrances or antibacterial agents can irritate your frog's sensitive skin.

2. Approach Gently: When you approach your frog, do so slowly and calmly. Sudden movements can startle it, leading to stress

or defensive behavior. Ensure the environment is quiet and calm to help keep your frog relaxed.

3. Use Both Hands: When picking up your Pacman frog, use both hands to support its body evenly. Place one hand under its belly and the other under its legs. This helps distribute the weight evenly and prevents injury. Be sure not to grip the frog too tightly; it should rest comfortably in your hands.

4. Avoid the Belly and Back: Don't handle your Pacman frog by its belly or back. Instead, support its body from underneath. Gripping by the belly or back can put unnecessary pressure on its organs, causing discomfort or harm.

5. Limit Handling Time: Pacman frogs don't like being handled too often. Frequent handling can stress them out. Limit each handling session to just a few minutes, and always watch how your frog reacts. If it tries to jump away or shows signs of stress, gently place it back in its habitat.

6. Avoid Contact with Water: When handling your Pacman frog, avoid getting it wet. Their skin is very sensitive and can absorb harmful substances from water. Make sure any handling is done in a dry area to protect your frog's health.

How Often Should You Handle Your Frog?

Pacman frogs are not the most social amphibians and don't need frequent handling. To keep your frog healthy and stress-free, it's best to limit how often you handle it.

1. How Often: You should handle your Pacman frog no more than once a week. This allows your frog to get used to being handled without getting too stressed out. Handling too often can make your frog anxious and may lead to health problems. Stick to a once-a-week schedule to keep your frog comfortable and happy.

2. How Long: When you do handle your frog, keep the sessions short—ideally, under 10 minutes. Pacman frogs can become overwhelmed if they are held for too long, which can interfere with their natural behavior and overall well-being. Short handling sessions help minimize stress and avoid disrupting their routine.

3. Watch for Stress: Always keep an eye on how your frog reacts to handling. Signs that your Pacman frog might be stressed include aggressive behavior, hiding more than usual, or a change in its eating habits. If you see any of these signs, it's a good idea to cut back on handling. The comfort and health of your frog should come before your desire for interaction.

Recognizing Stress In Your Frog

Taking care of your Pacman frog involves being alert to signs of stress. Stress can affect your frog's health and behavior in various ways, so it's essential to recognize these signs and respond appropriately.

1. Defensive Behavior: When a Pacman frog feels threatened, it may exhibit defensive behaviors. This includes puffing up its body, opening its mouth wide, or

trying to bite. These actions are attempts to protect itself from perceived dangers. If you notice these behaviors, it's a sign that your frog is stressed and uncomfortable.

2. Excessive Hiding: Pacman frogs are natural burrowers and will often hide. However, if you observe that your frog is hiding much more than usual or seems very reluctant to come out, it could be a sign of stress. Ensure that its hiding spots are suitable and not causing discomfort. It's important to check if the hiding spots are clean and if there's anything in the environment that might be making your frog uneasy.

3. Changes in Appetite: A sudden loss of appetite or refusal to eat can be a clear indicator of stress or other health issues. Monitor your frog's eating habits closely. If

your frog suddenly stops eating or eats much less than usual, this could signal a problem. If these changes persist, it's a good idea to consult a veterinarian to determine if there's an underlying issue that needs attention.

4. Physical Symptoms: Stress can also manifest as physical changes. Look out for any changes in your frog's skin color, the presence of unusual lumps, or any swelling. These physical symptoms might indicate stress or a health problem that requires immediate attention. Regularly check your frog's overall condition and seek veterinary advice if you notice anything unusual.

5. Behavioral Changes: Pay attention to any changes in your frog's behavior. Increased aggression or unusual lethargy can be signs of stress. Review how often you handle

your frog and check if the environmental conditions (like temperature and humidity) are appropriate. Adjusting these factors might help reduce stress and improve your frog's well-being.

☐

CHAPTER SEVEN

HEALTH AND WELLNESS

Common Health Issues

Pacman frogs, known for their unique looks and relatively easy care, can still face some common health issues that every owner should know about. Here's a simple guide to help you understand and manage these problems:

Skin Infections: Pacman frogs are prone to skin infections, often caused by poor tank hygiene, wrong humidity levels, or injuries. If you notice your frog's skin becoming red, swollen, or shedding unusually, it might be an infection. To prevent this, keep the tank clean and make sure the humidity is at the right level.

Metabolic Bone Disease (MBD): This condition happens when a Pacman frog doesn't get enough calcium in its diet. Calcium is crucial for healthy bones. Without it, the frog's bones can become soft or misshapen, and it may have trouble moving. You might notice a deformed jaw or a curved spine. To avoid MBD, dust your frog's food with a calcium supplement before feeding.

Respiratory Infections: These infections are common if the tank has too much humidity or poor ventilation. Look out for signs like labored breathing, mucus around the nose, or unusual tiredness. To help prevent respiratory problems, ensure your frog's tank is well-ventilated and avoid excessive moisture.

Parasites: Both external parasites like mites and internal ones like worms can affect Pacman frogs. Symptoms might include weight loss, strange stools, or itching. Regularly check your frog for any signs of parasites and consult a vet if you think your frog might have an infestation.

Signs Of A Healthy Frog

A healthy Pacman frog shows several clear signs that it is well. Here's what to look for to ensure your frog is in good shape:

1. Smooth, Vibrant Skin

A healthy Pacman frog has smooth, soft skin with no cuts, sores, or lumps. Its skin color should be bright and even. This brightness means the frog is well-hydrated. If the skin appears dull or has unusual spots, it could be a sign of health issues.

2. Clear, Bright Eyes

The eyes of a healthy Pacman frog are clear and bright, not cloudy or sunken. Sunken or cloudy eyes may suggest dehydration or illness.

3. Active and Alert

A healthy Pacman frog is active and alert, especially when it comes to feeding. If your frog seems sluggish or less responsive than usual, it might be sick or stressed.

4. Firm, Well-Proportioned Body

The frog's body should be firm and balanced, not swollen or oddly shaped. A healthy frog has a proportionate body without unusual lumps or bumps.

5. Normal Appetite and Steady Weight

A healthy Pacman frog has a good appetite and maintains a steady weight. If the frog is eating less or more than usual, or if it is losing or gaining weight rapidly, it could be a sign of a problem.

6. Regular Waste Production

The waste produced by a healthy Pacman frog should be regular and well-formed. Consistent waste helps indicate that the frog is digesting food properly and that its metabolism is functioning well.

7. Proper Shedding

Frogs shed their skin periodically, and this is normal. A healthy Pacman frog sheds its skin in small, manageable pieces. If your frog is shedding in large pieces or not shedding at all, it may be experiencing issues with humidity or overall health. Proper shedding is essential for growth and maintaining healthy skin.

Preventative Care

Keeping your Pacman frog healthy involves several important steps. The first step is to maintain a clean living environment. Regularly remove any uneaten food and waste from the tank to prevent harmful bacteria from growing. Clean the tank and replace the substrate as needed to ensure a sanitary space for your frog.

Humidity is crucial for your frog's well-being. You should keep the humidity in the tank between 60-80%. A hygrometer is a useful tool to help you monitor these levels. Additionally, always provide a water dish filled with fresh, dechlorinated water. Make sure to change the water regularly to keep it clean and safe for your frog.

Feeding is another key part of preventative care. Offer a balanced diet that includes live insects like crickets, mealworms, and dubia roaches. Occasionally dust the insects with calcium powder to ensure your frog gets the nutrients it needs. Be careful not to overfeed your frog, as obesity can lead to various health problems.

Regular visits to a veterinarian who specializes in amphibians are also important. A vet can help monitor your frog's health and catch any potential issues early. Routine health check-ups, including fecal exams, are useful for identifying parasites before they become serious.

Handling your Pacman frog should be kept to a minimum. Amphibians are sensitive to the oils and residues on human skin, which can cause skin problems. If you need to handle your frog, make sure your hands are clean and wet. This helps avoid harming your frog and keeps its skin in good condition.

CHAPTER EIGHT

DEALING WITH ILLNESS

Recognizing Early Signs Of Illness

Pacman Frogs are usually tough little creatures, but they can still get sick. Catching any signs of illness early can help you treat them more effectively. Here's what to look out for:

Change in Behavior: If your Pacman Frog suddenly becomes very sleepy or stops eating, it could be a sign that something is wrong. These frogs are normally active and have a good appetite. So, if you notice a change in these behaviors, it might be time to pay closer attention.

Skin Changes: A healthy Pacman Frog has smooth and moist skin. If you see that their skin looks dull, has rough patches, or changes color, this might indicate a skin infection or other health problems. Healthy skin is a good sign of overall well-being, so any changes here should not be ignored.

Abnormal Stool: Keep an eye on your frog's stool. If you notice diarrhea or if your frog isn't having bowel movements as usual, it could mean there's a problem with their digestive system. Normal stool is a sign of good health, so any changes can be important indicators.

Breathing Difficulties: Frogs use both their skin and lungs to breathe. If your Pacman Frog is having trouble breathing, such as breathing heavily or if you see bubbles around their nose and mouth, it's important to act quickly. Respiratory issues can be serious and need prompt attention.

Swelling: Watch for any swelling in your frog's body or limbs. Swelling might indicate fluid buildup or other serious health issues. If you see any unexplained swelling, it could be a sign of something more serious and should be investigated.

Loss of Appetite: If your Pacman Frog isn't eating for several days, it could be a sign of illness. These frogs normally have a strong appetite, so a sudden loss of interest in food can indicate a problem. Pay close attention to their eating habits and seek help if you notice they're not eating as usual.

Common Diseases And Treatments

Pacman Frogs, like all amphibians, can face several health issues. Knowing about these common diseases and how to treat them can help you keep your frog healthy and happy. Here's a guide to some typical problems and their solutions:

1. Fungal Infections: Fungal infections are a common concern for Pacman Frogs. You might notice skin lesions, discoloration, or peeling. To treat fungal infections, start by improving the cleanliness of the tank. Regularly change the water and use antifungal medications designed specifically for amphibians. Keeping the habitat clean and maintaining the right humidity levels can also help prevent these infections.

2. Bacterial Infections: Bacterial infections can cause skin ulcers or sores on your frog. These infections need to be treated with antibiotics. It's important to separate the infected frog from others to

avoid spreading the disease. Consult with a veterinarian to get the right medication and ensure the frog gets proper care.

3. Parasitic Infections: Your Pacman Frog might get parasites like internal worms or external mites. Symptoms include weight loss, visible worms in the feces, or itching. To address parasitic infections, use deworming medications or topical treatments. Regular deworming and keeping the habitat clean can help prevent these issues.

4. Metabolic Bone Disease (MBD): MBD is a condition that can occur if your frog doesn't get enough calcium or vitamin D3. Signs of MBD include deformities and difficulty moving. To prevent MBD, provide a proper diet with calcium supplements and UVB lighting. If MBD

develops, improve the diet and supplement it with the right nutrients.

5. Respiratory Infections: If your Pacman Frog shows signs of breathing difficulties, it may have a respiratory infection. Treatments for respiratory infections involve improving the frog's environment and possibly using antibiotics. Make sure the habitat has the correct humidity and temperature to help your frog recover.

When To See A Veterinarian

Knowing when to take your frog to the vet is important for their health and well-being. Here are some key signs that it's time to seek professional help from a veterinarian who specializes in reptiles or amphibians:

1. Persistent Symptoms: If you notice that your frog is showing symptoms like being unusually tired, not eating, or having problems with its skin for more than a few days, it's time to see a vet. These ongoing issues could indicate an underlying health problem that needs professional evaluation.

2. Severe Symptoms: If your frog has severe symptoms, you need to get veterinary help right away. This includes situations where your frog has noticeable swelling, trouble breathing, or is bleeding a lot. These symptoms could be signs of a serious condition that requires immediate attention from a vet.

3. Unresponsive to Home Treatments: Sometimes, you might try to treat your frog's condition at home by changing its

habitat or using over-the-counter remedies. If these efforts do not help and your frog's condition doesn't improve, it's important to consult a vet. A veterinarian can provide more advanced diagnostics and treatments that might be needed to address the problem effectively.

4. Uncertain Diagnosis: If you're unsure about what's wrong with your frog or what the best treatment might be, a vet can offer valuable guidance. They can help determine the correct diagnosis and recommend appropriate treatments. This is especially important if you're confused about whether the symptoms are normal or if they indicate a serious issue.

CHAPTER NINE

BREEDING PACMAN FROGS

Understanding Breeding Behavior

Pacman frogs (Ceratophrys spp.) are fascinating creatures from South America, known for their distinctive breeding behaviors. In their natural habitat, these frogs breed during the rainy season, which is a critical time for them to find mates and reproduce. To successfully breed Pacman frogs in captivity, it's important to mimic their natural environment as closely as possible.

Breeding for Pacman frogs usually happens when the rainy season begins. During this time, they become very active and start looking for potential mates. Male Pacman frogs have a unique way of attracting females. They produce a low, distinctive croak that can be heard from a distance. This croak is a signal that the male is ready to mate. When a female hears this call and is interested, she will respond, and the mating process begins.

The mating position for Pacman frogs is called amplexus. In this position, the male clasps onto the female's back. This grasp is important because it helps the male fertilize the eggs as they are laid. The amplexus position ensures that the eggs are fertilized right at the moment they are released.

For successful breeding, it's essential that both frogs are healthy and in good condition. Before you start the breeding process, make sure that your Pacman frogs are well-fed and of the right age. Typically, Pacman frogs reach sexual maturity between 2 and 3 years of age. At this point, they are ready to begin mating.

In captivity, recreating the rainy season environment can help stimulate breeding behavior. This might involve adjusting humidity levels and providing a suitable breeding area that mimics their natural habitat. Regularly monitoring the health and well-being of your frogs is crucial. They should be kept in a clean, comfortable environment with proper nutrition to ensure they are in the best condition for breeding.

Setting Up A Breeding Tank

Creating the right environment is crucial for encouraging Pacman frogs to breed. Here's a simple guide to setting up an ideal breeding tank for these fascinating creatures:

Tank Size and Setup

Start with a spacious tank to ensure your frogs have plenty of room. A 20-gallon tank is usually adequate for a pair of Pacman frogs. Make sure the tank has a secure lid. Pacman frogs are known for their ability to escape, so a well-fitting lid is essential to keep them safe and contained.

Substrate

Choose a substrate that keeps the tank moist but not overly wet. Coconut fiber or sphagnum moss are excellent choices. These materials help maintain the necessary humidity levels and create a more natural environment for the frogs. Avoid substrates that stay too soggy, as this can lead to health issues.

Water and Humidity

Pacman frogs need high humidity to stay healthy. Aim for a humidity level of 80% to 90% inside the tank. You can achieve this by using a misting system or regularly spraying the tank with water. It's also a good idea to have a hygrometer to measure the humidity accurately. Place a shallow water dish in the tank where the frogs can soak. Make sure the water is dechlorinated, as chlorine can be harmful to your frogs.

Temperature

Maintaining the right temperature is key to creating a comfortable environment for your frogs. Keep the temperature in the tank between 75°F and 85°F (24°C to 29°C). You can use a heat lamp or heating pad to regulate the temperature, but be careful not to place these directly under the tank, as this can create hot spots that may stress your frogs.

Additional Hides

Provide plenty of hiding spots to help reduce stress and make your frogs feel secure. Use caves, large pieces of bark, or other natural decorations. These hiding places give the frogs a sense of safety and help them feel more at ease in their tank.

Breeding Conditions

To encourage breeding, simulate conditions that mimic the rainy season. Increase the humidity and create a slight drop in temperature to replicate the changes that occur in nature. These adjustments can help trigger the breeding behavior in your Pacman frogs.

Caring For Eggs And Tadpoles

After Pacman frogs breed, your focus shifts to taking care of their eggs and tadpoles to ensure they grow into healthy frogs.

Eggs: Pacman frog eggs are laid in water and look like small, round, gelatinous clumps. To prevent problems like mold or fungus, keep the tank clean by removing any leftover food or waste. It's essential to maintain high humidity and ensure the water is clean and free from contaminants.

Tadpoles: A few days after the eggs are laid, they will hatch into tadpoles. At this stage, you need to provide a gentle filtration system to keep the water clean. Avoid strong water currents, as they can stress the tadpoles.

Feeding: Tadpoles initially eat algae and tiny microorganisms in the tank. As they grow, you can start giving them powdered tadpole food or finely crushed fish flakes. Be careful not to overfeed them, as too much food can cause the water quality to decline, which can harm the tadpoles.

Metamorphosis: As tadpoles develop into froglets, they will start to change. You will see their legs forming and their tails getting shorter. Provide a shallow water area with some dry land where the froglets can climb out. This helps them adjust to life outside the water.

Transitioning: Once the froglets have completed metamorphosis, they can be moved to a habitat suitable for adult Pacman frogs. Make sure their new home has the right humidity and temperature to keep them comfortable.

CHAPTER TEN

SEASONAL CARE AND ADJUSTMENTS

Adapting To Different Seasons

Pacman Frogs, originally from South America, are accustomed to a variety of temperatures and weather conditions throughout the year. Despite their tough nature, these frogs still need a little assistance from their owners to adapt to the changing seasons. In their natural habitat, Pacman Frogs experience different temperatures and humidity levels as the seasons change. In your home, it's important to mimic these conditions to keep your frog healthy and comfortable. Here's how you can help your Pacman Frog adjust to different seasons.

1. Temperature Control:

Pacman Frogs thrive in temperatures ranging from 75°F to 85°F (24°C to 29°C). During warmer months, your home may naturally be within this range, but as temperatures drop in the fall and winter, you may need to provide additional warmth. Use a heat lamp or a heat mat to maintain the proper temperature. Make sure to check the temperature regularly with a thermometer to ensure it stays within the recommended range.

2. Humidity Levels:

Humidity is another important factor for your Pacman Frog's well-being. In their natural environment, these frogs are accustomed to high humidity. Aim to keep the humidity level in their enclosure between 60% and 80%. During the dry winter months, indoor air can become quite dry. To combat this, use a humidifier or mist the enclosure regularly to maintain the proper humidity level.

3. Habitat Adjustments:

Adapting your frog's habitat to the changing seasons can also involve adjusting the substrate and providing additional hiding spots. In colder months, consider using a substrate that retains moisture well, such as sphagnum moss, to help maintain humidity. Adding extra hides can provide your frog with secure places to retreat, which can be especially comforting during seasonal changes.

4. Dietary Considerations:

Although Pacman Frogs generally have a hearty appetite, their feeding habits might change with the seasons. Monitor their eating patterns and adjust their diet if needed. During colder months, their metabolism may slow down, so they might eat less frequently.

Winter Care: Hibernation And Brumation

During the winter, Pacman Frogs enter a state called brumation, which is similar to hibernation but slightly different. Brumation is when a frog's metabolism slows down significantly due to the colder temperatures. As the weather gets cooler, your Pacman Frog will become less active and may not eat as much.

Here's how you can help your Pacman Frog stay healthy during brumation:

1. Adjust Temperature: Keep your frog's enclosure at a steady temperature between 70-75°F (21-24°C). It's important not to let the temperature drop below 65°F (18°C), as this could cause health issues. Make sure to use a reliable thermometer to monitor the temperature and keep it consistent.

2. Humidity Levels: Maintain high humidity in the enclosure, ideally around 60-80%. This helps prevent dehydration, which can be a concern when the frog's activity levels decrease. Use a hygrometer to check the humidity levels regularly. If needed, mist the enclosure with water to keep the humidity high. You can also add a shallow water dish to help with humidity and hydration.

3. Feeding: During brumation, your Pacman Frog will eat less, and that's completely normal. Reduce the frequency of feeding to every 7-10 days instead of the usual routine. Offer small amounts of food when you do feed, and monitor your frog to see if it shows interest in eating. It's important not to overfeed or force food if your frog isn't hungry.

4. Enclosure: Make sure the enclosure is secure and well-insulated. Avoid placing it in drafty areas or near windows where temperature changes can occur. A stable environment is key to keeping your frog comfortable and healthy during brumation. Check the enclosure regularly to ensure that it remains at the proper temperature and humidity levels.

☐

Summer Care: Heat And Hydration

In the warmer months, your Pacman Frog will become more active and have a faster metabolism. This means it will eat more and need extra care for its hydration and temperature needs. Here's how to keep your Pacman Frog healthy and comfortable during summer:

Temperature

Increase the temperature in your frog's enclosure to between 75-80°F (24-27°C). Make sure the enclosure has a temperature gradient so your frog can move between warmer and cooler areas as needed. You can use a heat lamp or heating pad to help maintain this temperature range. This allows your frog to regulate its body temperature by choosing the area that feels right.

Humidity Levels

Keep the humidity high, ideally around 60-80%. This helps your frog stay hydrated and maintain its skin health. You may need to mist the enclosure more frequently during the summer, especially if the air in your home is dry. Using a humidity gauge will help you monitor the levels and ensure they stay within the right range.

Feeding

Your Pacman Frog will have a bigger appetite during the warmer months. Feed it more often, about every 2-3 days. Offer a variety of foods, such as insects and other suitable prey items, to provide balanced nutrition. Monitor your frog's eating habits to ensure it's getting enough food and adjust the amount if needed.

Water

Always provide a shallow dish of fresh, clean water in the enclosure. This water dish should be available at all times to help your frog stay hydrated. It also gives your frog a place to soak if it needs to. Make sure to change the water regularly and clean the dish to prevent any buildup of bacteria or mold.

General Tips For All Seasons

Taking care of your frog involves some essential practices that apply no matter the time of year. Here are some straightforward tips to help you keep your frog healthy and happy throughout the seasons:

1. Regular Monitoring

Always keep a close eye on your frog's health and behavior. This means observing how active they are, how much they eat, and whether they look healthy. If you notice any changes—such as a drop in activity, a change in appetite, or unusual physical appearances—these could be signs of health issues. Early detection of problems can help you address them before they become more serious. Regular check-ups and paying attention to your frog's habits are crucial for maintaining their well-being.

2. Cleanliness

Maintaining a clean living environment for your frog is very important. A clean tank helps prevent the buildup of waste and harmful bacteria that could lead to health problems. Make sure to regularly clean and disinfect the enclosure. This involves removing old, soiled substrate and replacing it with fresh, clean material. Regular cleaning will help keep your frog's habitat sanitary and reduce the risk of infections and diseases.

3. Lighting

Proper lighting is necessary to mimic the natural day and night cycle for your frog. While Pacman Frogs, for example, don't require UVB lighting like some reptiles do, they still benefit from a regular light schedule. Providing a consistent light and dark cycle helps regulate their natural rhythms and can contribute to their overall health. Make sure the lighting setup is suitable for your frog's specific needs and adjust as necessary to maintain a balanced environment.

CHAPTER ELEVEN

TANK MAINTENANCE

Regular Cleaning Schedule

Maintaining a clean environment is crucial for keeping your Pacman Frog healthy. Here's a simple guide to help you set up an effective cleaning routine:

Daily Tasks:

1. Check for Waste: Every day, look inside the tank for any waste or leftover food. Pacman Frogs can be quite messy, and uneaten food can quickly decompose. This can lead to poor water quality and health issues for your frog.

2. Remove Debris: Use a small net or tweezers to pick up any visible waste, leftover food, or other debris. Removing

these helps keep the tank clean and prevents the growth of harmful bacteria.

Weekly Tasks:

1.   Partial Water Change: Once a week, replace about 25-30% of the tank's water. Be sure to use dechlorinated or distilled water. This helps keep the water clean and reduces the buildup of waste products, which can be harmful to your frog.

2.   Clean the Substrate: If you use soil or coconut fiber as substrate, it's important to keep it clean. Gently stir the substrate to prevent mold and bacteria from forming. If any parts of the substrate look dirty or smell bad, replace them with fresh material.

Monthly Tasks:

1. Deep Clean: Once a month, do a thorough cleaning of the tank. First, move your Pacman Frog to a temporary container with water from its tank. Then, remove all decorations, substrate, and equipment from the tank. Wash the tank with mild soap and water, rinse it thoroughly, and let it dry completely before putting everything back in.

2. Inspect Equipment: Check all equipment, including the heater, filter, and lighting. Make sure everything is working properly. Clean the equipment if needed and replace any worn-out or malfunctioning parts.

Managing Mold And Fungus

Mold and fungus can become a problem in your Pacman Frog's tank, especially if it's too humid. It's important to address these issues quickly to keep your frog healthy. Here's a simple guide on how to manage mold and fungus in your frog's environment.

How to Identify Mold and Fungus

1. Appearance: Mold often looks like fuzzy, discolored patches on the substrate (like the material on the tank floor), decorations, or even on the tank itself. Fungus can appear as white or grayish spots.

2. Smell: If you notice a sour or musty smell coming from the tank, it could be a sign of mold or fungus.

How to Prevent Mold and Fungus

1. Maintain Proper Humidity: Keep the humidity in your Pacman Frog's tank at the

right level. Ideal humidity for a Pacman Frog is around 70-80%. Use a hygrometer to check and maintain this humidity level. Proper humidity helps prevent mold and fungus growth.

2. Good Ventilation: Ensure the tank has good air circulation to avoid stagnant air, which can contribute to mold growth. However, don't place the tank in drafty areas as this can affect the tank's temperature stability.

How to Treat Mold and Fungus

1. Remove Contaminated Areas: If you find mold or fungus, immediately take out the affected substrate or decorations. Clean these items thoroughly or replace them if they are too contaminated.

2. **Use Antifungal Solutions:** For serious cases, you might need to use an antifungal solution. Make sure the antifungal product you choose is safe for amphibians and follow the instructions carefully.

3. **Improve Tank Conditions:** Adjust the tank's humidity and temperature to create an environment that's less likely to foster mold and fungus. Regular cleaning and maintenance will also help prevent these issues from recurring.

Safe Handling Of Waste And Uneaten Food

Maintaining a clean and safe environment for your Pacman Frog involves proper handling of waste and uneaten food. Here are some guides to help you manage these tasks effectively:

Removing Waste

1.   Use the Right Tools: To keep things hygienic, use a small scoop, net, or tweezers to pick up waste from the tank. Avoid using your hands directly. This minimizes the risk of spreading bacteria and keeps the process sanitary.

2.   Proper Disposal: Once you've collected the waste, place it in a sealed bag. This not only helps to contain any unpleasant odors but also prevents the waste from contaminating other areas. Proper disposal is key to maintaining a clean tank and ensuring your frog's habitat remains healthy.

Handling Uneaten Food

1.   Regular Checks: Make it a habit to inspect the tank frequently for any uneaten

food. Pacman Frogs may not finish their meals, and leftover food can become a problem quickly. Regular checks ensure that any food left behind is noticed in time.

2. Timely Removal: Remove any uneaten food as soon as possible, ideally within a few hours. This prevents the food from rotting or spoiling, which can lead to contamination. Spoiled food can also attract pests, and it can negatively affect the quality of the tank's environment. Prompt removal helps keep the tank clean and reduces the risk of health issues for your frog.

CHAPTER TWELVE

ENRICHMENT AND STIMULATION

Environmental Enrichment

Keeping Pacman frogs healthy and happy involves providing a stimulating environment that closely mimics their natural habitat. These fascinating frogs are known for their large mouths and mostly sedentary behavior, so they benefit greatly from an enriched living space. Environmental enrichment helps them stay active and reduces stress by encouraging natural behaviors.

To create a comfortable and engaging habitat for your Pacman frog, start with a well-structured terrarium. The enclosure should have plenty of hiding spots, which can be made from rocks, logs, and plants.

These hiding places give your frog a sense of security and allow it to establish its own territory. Since Pacman frogs are used to damp environments, the substrate in their terrarium should be kept moist. Materials like coconut fiber or sphagnum moss are excellent choices because they help maintain the right level of humidity and offer a surface where the frog can dig.

Including live plants in the terrarium can enhance the frog's environment in several ways. Plants like ferns and bromeliads not only make the habitat look more natural but also provide extra hiding spots and help regulate humidity. It's important to choose plants that are safe for frogs, ensuring they won't harm your pet if they happen to eat them.

Another key component of your Pacman frog's habitat is a shallow water dish. Frogs need access to clean water for drinking and soaking, so the dish should be large enough for the frog to fully submerge itself but shallow enough to prevent drowning. Regularly change the water to keep it clean and free from bacteria or other contaminants.

Mental Stimulation Techniques

Keeping your Pacman frog mentally stimulated is essential for its well-being, even though these frogs aren't as active as some other species. Providing mental challenges can help reduce stress and keep your frog engaged. Here are some easy ways to stimulate your Pacman frog.

1. Food Enrichment: One effective method to engage your Pacman frog is through

food enrichment. Change up its diet by offering a variety of live prey such as crickets, worms, and small fish. Instead of always placing the food in the same spot, try placing it in different locations within the enclosure. This variation encourages your frog to use its natural hunting instincts.

Using feeding tongs can add an extra layer of interaction. Move the food around with the tongs so your Pacman frog has to actively hunt and respond to the movement. This activity not only makes feeding time more stimulating but also helps your frog stay physically and mentally active.

2. Scent Trails: Another way to keep your Pacman frog mentally engaged is by using scent trails. This technique involves

creating a trail with the scent of food items to encourage exploration. To do this, drag a food item or a piece of prey across the substrate in your frog's enclosure. This will leave a scent trail for your frog to follow.

By following the scent trail, your Pacman frog will use its sense of smell to find the food, which simulates natural foraging behavior. This method can help stimulate your frog's natural instincts and encourage it to explore different parts of its enclosure.

3. Changing the Environment: You can also keep your Pacman frog mentally stimulated by occasionally changing its environment. Rearrange the items in the enclosure or add new elements like different types of hiding spots or decorations. This change in the environment can make the enclosure more

interesting and encourage your frog to explore.

4. Interactive Toys: Some pet owners find that adding simple, safe interactive toys can also provide mental stimulation. For instance, small objects that move or make noise when touched can intrigue your Pacman frog and encourage it to interact with its surroundings.

Creating A Naturalistic Environment

Creating a naturalistic environment for your Pacman frog is important for its well-being. In the wild, Pacman frogs live in the rainforests of South America, where they thrive in moist, dense vegetation with lots of hiding spots. To make your frog feel more at home in captivity, you should try to replicate these conditions as closely as possible.

Start by setting up a terrarium that resembles a rainforest. Use a variety of plants, rocks, and natural materials to create a habitat that mimics the frog's natural environment. Choose plants that can thrive in high humidity and provide plenty of hiding spots, as Pacman frogs like to feel secure.

It's crucial to maintain the right humidity and temperature in the terrarium. Pacman frogs need a temperature range between 75-80°F during the day, with a slightly cooler temperature at night. You can use a heating pad or a ceramic heater to keep the temperature steady, but be sure to monitor it carefully to avoid overheating.

Humidity is equally important for your frog's health. To keep the humidity levels consistent, consider adding a misting system to the terrarium. Regular misting will help maintain proper humidity and add moisture to the environment, which is essential for your frog's comfort.

In addition to setting up the right environment, pay close attention to your Pacman frog's behavior. Observe how it interacts with its habitat and make adjustments as needed. Every frog is unique, so what works for one might not work for another. If you notice your frog seems stressed or uncomfortable, try changing the setup or adding new elements to better suit its needs.

CHAPTER THIRTEEN

TRAVELING WITH YOUR PACMAN FROG

Preparing For Travel

Traveling with your Pacman frog requires careful planning to ensure your pet's comfort and safety. Here's how you can prepare:

1. Travel Container: Select a small, secure, and well-ventilated container for your Pacman frog. The container should be big enough for your frog to move around comfortably but not too large, as a spacious container could lead to injuries. Make sure the lid is secure to prevent your frog from escaping.

2. Substrate: Line the bottom of the container with a suitable substrate. Damp paper towels or a moist sponge work well

for keeping the environment comfortable. Avoid substrates like gravel or sand, as these can be harmful if your frog ingests them or if they cause injury.

3. Temperature Control: Pacman frogs are sensitive to temperature changes, so it's important to keep the temperature stable during travel. Use a heat pack to keep the container warm or a cooler to avoid overheating. Check the temperature regularly to make sure it stays within a safe range.

4. Water Supply: Include a small, shallow dish of clean water in the container. Make sure the water is treated to remove chlorine or other harmful chemicals. If a dish isn't practical, a damp cloth can help maintain humidity in the container.

5. Food and Supplements: If your trip will be long, bring some of your Pacman frog's regular food in a small container. It's best not to feed your frog just before traveling to minimize stress-related issues.

6. Health Check: Before you travel, make sure your Pacman frog is healthy. If you have any concerns about your frog's health, consult a veterinarian who specializes in amphibians.

Ensuring Safety During Transit

When traveling with your Pacman frog, your main goal is to keep it safe and as relaxed as possible. Here's how you can ensure a smooth trip:

1. Secure Handling: Be very careful with the travel container. Handle it gently and avoid any sudden movements that might scare your frog. Place the container on a

stable surface where it won't shift around. Make sure the container is not exposed to direct sunlight or extreme temperatures, as this can harm your frog.

2. Monitoring Conditions: Regularly check the conditions inside the container to make sure they are just right for your frog. This includes checking the temperature, humidity, and water levels. If you notice that any of these conditions are off, make the necessary adjustments to keep your frog comfortable. Keeping track of these factors will help prevent stress and health issues for your frog.

3. Avoiding Stress: Try to keep your frog's environment as calm as possible. Avoid loud noises, bright lights, and sudden changes in the environment, all of which can stress out your frog. If you are

traveling by car, keep the volume of the music low and avoid making sudden stops or sharp turns. These actions will help in keeping your frog calm and comfortable throughout the journey.

4. Handling Emergencies: Be prepared for any emergencies that might come up during the trip. Have a basic first-aid kit with you, including items like antiseptic, bandages, and any medications your frog might need. It's also a good idea to know where the nearest veterinary facilities are, just in case you need professional help quickly.

5. Rest Stops: If your trip is long, make sure to plan for regular rest stops. Use these breaks to check on your Pacman frog and make sure everything is okay. During these stops, you can also inspect the travel

container's conditions and make any necessary adjustments. This will help ensure that your frog remains safe and comfortable throughout the journey.

Post-Travel Care

Once you arrive at your destination with your Pacman frog, it's important to take a few steps to help it adjust and recover from the journey.

1. Settling In: First, place the travel container with your Pacman frog in a quiet and secure spot. This should be somewhere safe where your frog can get used to its new surroundings without any disturbances. Avoid handling your frog right after the trip; this will help minimize its stress.

2. Environmental Setup: Before moving your Pacman frog into its new home, make sure the habitat is properly set up. This

includes preparing the right substrate (bedding material), setting the correct temperature and humidity levels, and ensuring there is a fresh water supply. It's crucial to have everything ready so your frog can move into a comfortable and safe environment.

3. Health Check: Keep a close eye on your Pacman frog to spot any signs of stress or health problems. Look for any changes in its behavior, appetite, or physical appearance. If you notice anything unusual, such as changes in eating habits or physical symptoms like lethargy, consult a veterinarian right away.

4. Rehydration and Feeding: Once your frog is settled in, provide it with fresh water. If it's been a while since your frog last ate, you can offer a small amount of

food. However, be cautious not to overfeed it, as your frog might need some time to get used to its new environment and feeding routine.

5. Observation: Spend some time watching your Pacman frog in its new habitat. Check to see if it is adapting well and showing normal behavior. It's important to address any issues or concerns as soon as you spot them, to ensure a smooth transition and help your frog settle into its new home comfortably.

☐

CHAPTER FOURTEEN

LEGAL AND ETHICAL CONSIDERATIONS

Understanding Local Laws And Regulations

Keeping Pacman frogs as pets requires knowing and following local laws and regulations. These rules can vary a lot depending on where you live, and not following them can lead to legal trouble or even losing your pet.

First, many places have specific laws about owning exotic animals like Pacman frogs. It's important to check with your local wildlife or animal control office to find out if it's legal to keep a Pacman frog in your area. Some places might need special permits or licenses for exotic pets, while others might ban them altogether.

Next, there are often regulations about breeding and selling Pacman frogs. Some areas have strict rules to stop illegal wildlife trade and make sure that breeding is done responsibly. Make sure you understand these rules to avoid accidentally breaking any laws.

Environmental and conservation laws also matter. Some Pacman frog species might be protected by local or international conservation laws, especially if they are threatened or endangered. It's crucial to ensure that any Pacman frog you get has been sourced ethically and legally. This means buying from reputable breeders or sellers who can prove their frogs were obtained lawfully.

In addition, if you live in a place with laws about the breeding and sale of Pacman frogs, make sure you are aware of these regulations. They are designed to prevent illegal trade and ensure that animals are kept in good conditions. Not following these rules can result in fines or other legal consequences.

Before getting a Pacman frog, take the time to research and understand the specific regulations in your area. This will help you avoid potential legal problems and ensure that you are providing a safe and legal home for your new pet. Following local laws not only helps you stay out of trouble but also supports the ethical treatment of animals and helps protect wildlife.

Ethical Care Practices

Caring for your Pacman frog responsibly is essential for its health and happiness. Ethical care means going beyond basic needs and creating an environment that supports your frog's overall well-being.

1. Mimic Their Natural Habitat: Pacman frogs come from specific environments, so it's crucial to replicate their natural habitat in their enclosure. Research the exact temperature, humidity, and substrate (bedding) needs for your species. Make sure their habitat includes hiding spots, proper lighting, and an appropriate size to allow them to grow and exhibit natural behaviors.

2. Provide a Balanced Diet: Pacman frogs are carnivores, meaning they need a diet of live prey such as crickets, worms, and small rodents. It's important to offer a variety of food to ensure they get all the nutrients they need. Make sure the prey is the right

size for your frog and nutritionally balanced to keep them healthy.

3. Avoid Overbreeding: Responsible ownership means not contributing to overpopulation. Don't breed your Pacman frogs unless you have the experience and resources to care for the young. If you do decide to breed them, find suitable homes for the offspring and make sure they are well cared for.

4. Handle With Care: Pacman frogs can become stressed with too much handling. Limit how often you handle your frog and be gentle when you do. Excessive handling can lead to health problems and stress. Keep their habitat clean and free from dangers to avoid harming them.

The Importance Of Captive Breeding

Captive breeding is crucial for conserving and ethically managing Pacman frogs. When done right, it helps lessen the impact on wild populations and supports the overall health and survival of the species.

One major advantage of captive breeding is that it reduces the need to capture frogs from their natural habitats. Wild-caught frogs are often taken in large numbers, which can harm their populations and damage their environments. By breeding Pacman frogs in captivity, we can decrease the demand for wild specimens, thus protecting natural populations and reducing environmental harm. This approach also helps maintain genetic diversity within the species. Properly managed breeding programs can prevent inbreeding and ensure a healthier, more diverse gene pool.

Captive breeding provides a safer and more controlled environment for the frogs. In captivity, they are less exposed to diseases and threats that they might face in the wild. This controlled setting allows for close monitoring of their health, making it easier to provide the care they need. In a well-managed captive environment, the frogs can receive proper food, medical care, and attention, which contributes to their overall well-being.

Despite these benefits, captive breeding must be approached with care and responsibility. It is important to ensure that breeding practices are ethical and that the welfare of the frogs is a top priority. Breeding should not be driven by profit alone; the focus must be on the health and well-being of the animals. This means providing a good quality of life for the frogs and making sure they are not subjected to unnecessary stress or poor conditions.

CHAPTER FIFTEEN

TROUBLESHOOTING AND FAQS

Common Beginner Mistakes

Caring for a Pacman Frog can be a fulfilling and enjoyable experience, but many new owners make a few common mistakes. Knowing about these issues can help you avoid problems and provide the best care for your frog. Here's a look at some frequent errors and tips on how to avoid them:

1. Incorrect Habitat Setup: Setting up the right habitat is crucial for your Pacman Frog's well-being. A common mistake is not providing the correct environment. Pacman Frogs need a terrarium with specific humidity and temperature levels. Beginners often use the wrong type of substrate or fail to keep the humidity

where it needs to be. Use a substrate that retains moisture, like coconut fiber or sphagnum moss, and keep the humidity between 60% and 80%. A hygrometer can help you monitor these levels accurately.

2. Overfeeding or Underfeeding: Feeding your Pacman Frog properly is essential for its health. A common mistake is either overfeeding or underfeeding. Pacman Frogs have a big appetite and might eat too much if given the chance. On the other hand, not feeding them enough can lead to malnutrition. Offer a variety of appropriately sized insects, such as crickets or mealworms, and make sure the food is no larger than the width of your frog's head. Feed them once or twice a week to avoid overfeeding.

3. Inadequate Hiding Spots: Pacman Frogs are natural burrowers and need hiding spots to feel secure. Without these hiding places, they might get stressed. Provide several hiding spots in their terrarium. You can use frog hides from pet stores or make your own with pieces of bark or plastic containers. Make sure the hides are big enough for your frog to fit comfortably and feel safe.

4. Improper Water Conditions: Water quality is very important for your Pacman Frog's health. Some beginners use tap water directly, which can contain harmful chemicals like chlorine. Always treat tap water with a dechlorinator or use a water conditioner to make it safe. Keep the water dish clean and replace the water regularly to maintain a healthy environment.

5. Handling Issues: Pacman Frogs are not as interactive as some other types of pet frogs and can become stressed from too much handling. Avoid handling your frog too often or too roughly. If you need to move it, do so gently to avoid causing stress.

6. Temperature Fluctuations: Keeping the temperature stable is essential for your frog's health. Pacman Frogs need a temperature range of 75°F to 85°F (24°C to 29°C). Beginners sometimes use heat sources that don't maintain a consistent temperature or forget to use a thermometer. Invest in a reliable heating system and thermometer to ensure the temperature stays within the correct range.

7. Lack of Environmental Enrichment: A well-enriched environment helps mimic

the Pacman Frog's natural habitat. Some beginners overlook this need. Provide a substrate that allows for burrowing, and occasionally rearrange the habitat to keep it interesting. Adding live plants or logs can also make the environment more natural and engaging for your frog.

Frequently Asked Questions

1. How often should I feed my Pacman Frog?

Pacman Frogs need to be fed once or twice a week. They are known for their big appetites, so it's crucial to give them appropriately sized insects and avoid giving them too much food. Younger Pacman Frogs may need more frequent feedings, while adult frogs can be fed less often.

2. What type of substrate is best for my Pacman Frog?

For your Pacman Frog, it's best to use a substrate that retains moisture, like coconut fiber, sphagnum moss, or a mix of both. These substrates help keep the right humidity levels and allow your frog to burrow comfortably. Avoid using sand or gravel, as these materials can lead to health problems.

3. How do I keep the humidity level in the terrarium?

To keep the humidity levels in your Pacman Frog's terrarium, mist the enclosure regularly and use a humidity gauge to monitor the levels. You can also place a shallow dish of water inside the terrarium to help with humidity. If needed, use a humidity dome or a humidifier to maintain the right humidity levels.

4. Can I use tap water for my Pacman Frog?

Tap water often contains chemicals like chlorine that can be harmful to your Pacman Frog. It's important to use dechlorinated water or treat tap water with a water conditioner to remove these chemicals. Always clean and refill the water dish with fresh, treated water to keep your frog healthy.

5. What temperature should the terrarium be?

Pacman Frogs prefer temperatures between 75°F and 85°F (24°C to 29°C). To keep the temperature in this range, use a thermometer to check the temperature and a reliable heating source to maintain consistent warmth.

6. How can I tell if my Pacman Frog is sick?

If your Pacman Frog is sick, you might notice signs like lethargy (not being active), loss of appetite, changes in skin texture or color, or difficulty breathing. If you see any of these symptoms, it's important to take your frog to a veterinarian who has experience with amphibians.

7. How often should I clean the terrarium?

Cleaning the terrarium regularly is key to keeping your Pacman Frog healthy. Spot clean daily by removing waste and uneaten food. Every 1-2 weeks, do a thorough cleaning: change the substrate, wash the water dish, and clean the rest of the terrarium to prevent bacteria and maintain a clean environment.

THE END

Manufactured by Amazon.ca
Acheson, AB

14434854R00081